# FACEPOEMS

## Also by Fred Wallace

*Living Life Simply* (poems)
*Simply Living Life* (poems)
*Life-Affirming Fredkūs* (poems)

*A Well That Keeps Flowing—*
*The Power of Co-Counseling* (self-help)

Upcoming: *MAYDAY, 1971:*
*A Generation's Last Battle Against the Vietnam War*

# FACEPOEMS

*You've got an honest face*

Written and Illustrated by

# FRED WALLACE

ISBN: 978-0-9862231-1-2

Publisher: Be Your Greatness    Contact: earthfred@aol.com

Book Design and Production: wordsintheworks.com

*Dedication*

To my many friends who
bring joy to my heart
like the birds that return to
New England every spring.

*Hi, Dear Reader,*

Welcome to the world of *FacePoems* where feelings come alive.

You will see how each charming image and accompanying poem tells its own human story.

*FacePoems* will engage your spirits and awaken your emotions.

So turn the page to begin this journey of exploration and fun.

And if you happen to identify with one of the *FacePoems*, smile and be joyful.

Peace,

*Fred Wallace*

Sweetness warms my body;

Angels dance and sing in my soul.

Smiling comes naturally!

So sweet the smile

Of peaceful contentment.

Let exuberance reign.

Profound sadness inside,

Distorting natural beauty.

Let tears begin to flow.

So stern. So very stern.

Lighten up! Blink your eyes! Now smile;

Your frown will disappear.

Sweet thoughts come through my brain

When I first smell the lilacs.

Then I remove my shoes.

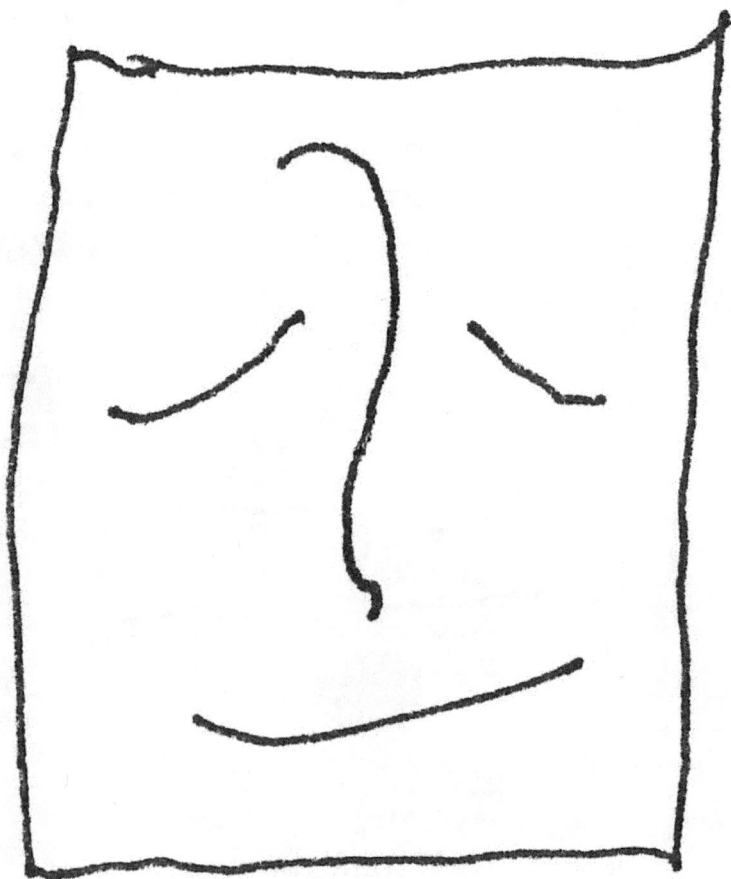

Wish you were
here today—
To play and dance
and sing with us.
We miss your
energy.

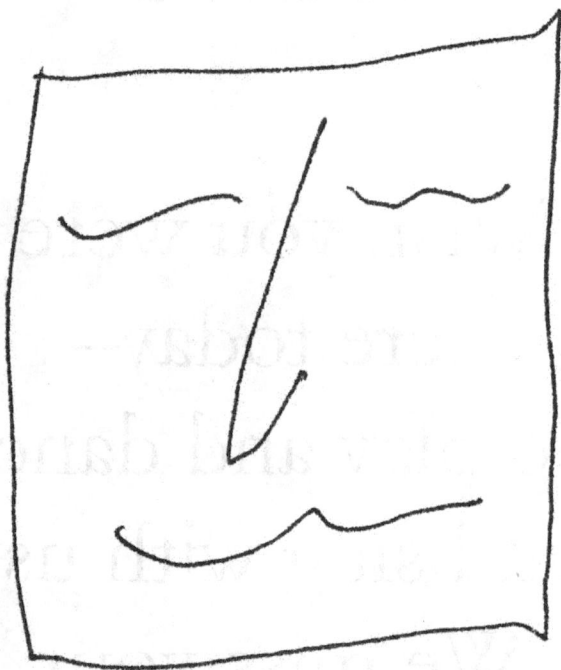

Don't believe what you see–

Just tell me what you are feeling.

My soul is blue and white

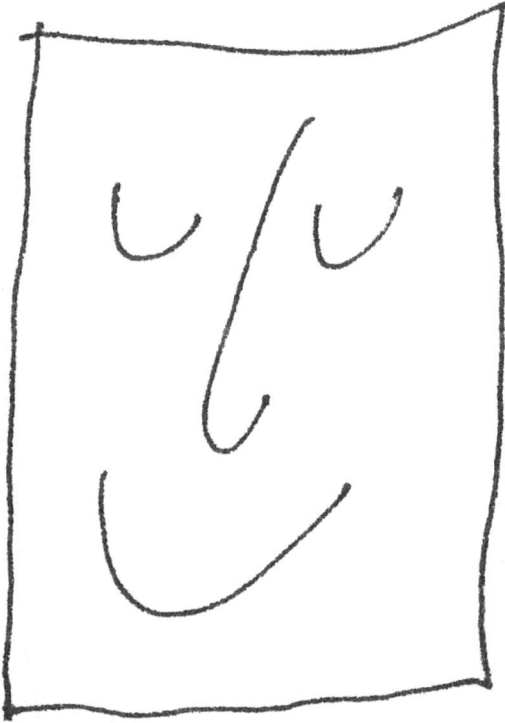

Ahhh, I'm growing older.

Contentment and peace have found me.

I smile every morning.

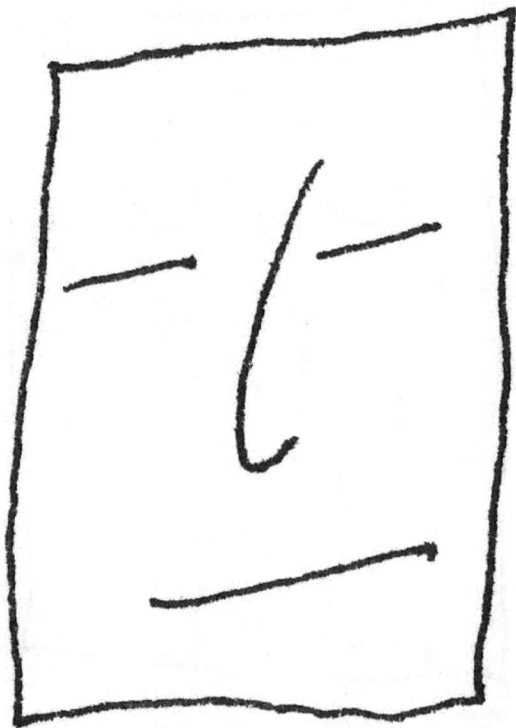

Not so happy am I,

Wondering what happens when I die.

But not so sad…I'm alive.

Joyful playful being;

Your smiling soul lights up your face.

Keep dancing your sweet dance.

Wondering what happened…

I'll tell you if you have the time.

I danced with love all night.

Everything is okay.

Life is good and I can dream dreams.

You wonder why I am smug?

Nothing! Nothing! Nothing!

I'm not even sure why I'm here.

I think I will go home.

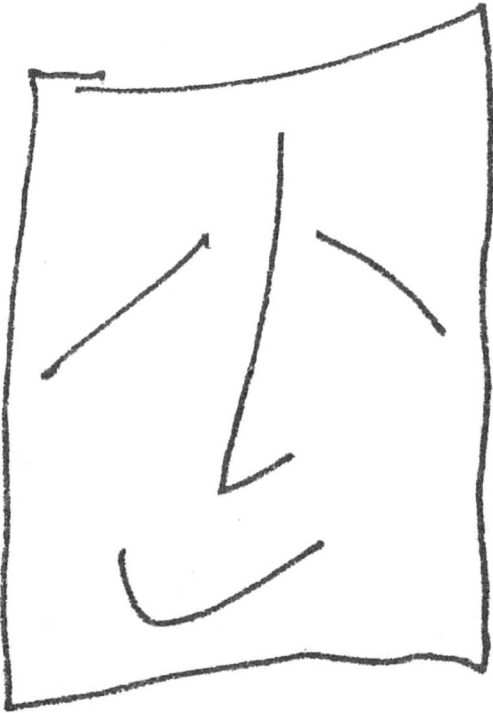

How sweet my life can be.

I lay my head on a pillow,

Close my eyes and dream dreams.

Grumbling old man,

Try a smile.

It won't hurt your face.

You tight-lipped talker—

Mumbling your way through ragged times.

Time to open your mouth!

Sad I am, I think,
but maybe not.
Time for a walk.

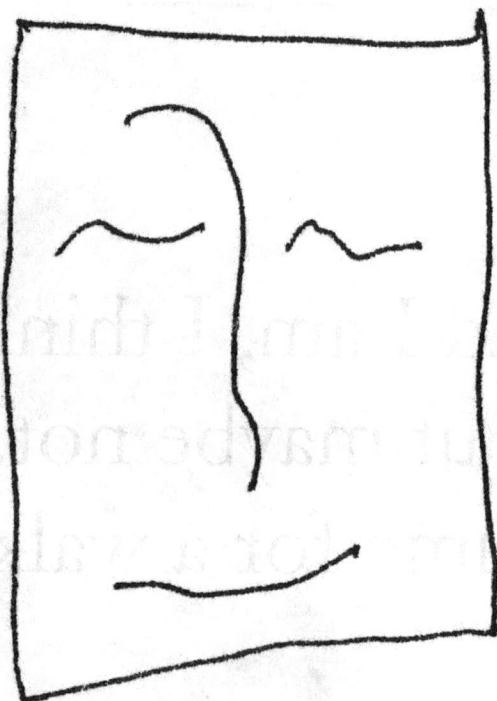

Playful thoughts fill my head,

Not fantasies about success,

But dancing in the office.

So it did not happen

The way you thought it would happen–

Let go and start over.

I knew you would show up;

I am so pleased that you are here.

May I have the next dance?

A puzzle I am–

To myself, and others.

Who am I?

Joy sneaks across your face,

You can't repress your soul's delight.

Open your mouth and laugh!

What lurks behind the face

So torn with anguish and fear?

Is there a young child's pain?

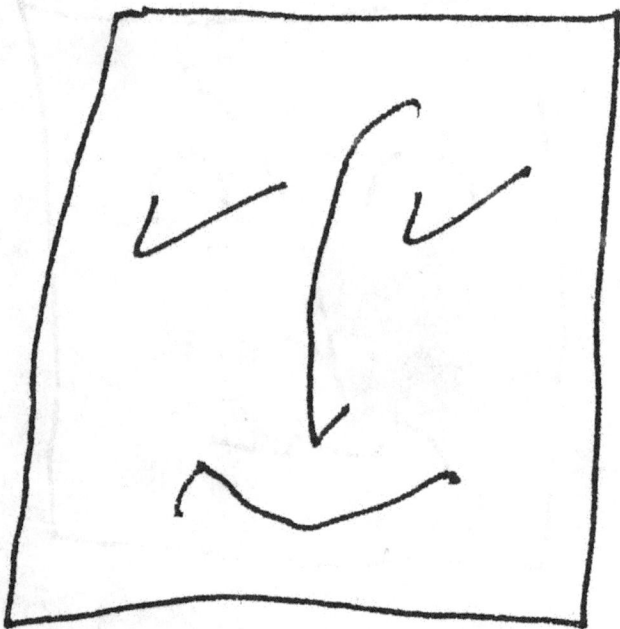

I need to caress my dream.

No one needs to know what it is—

My dream brings me joy.

What mysteries I know;

Intriguing and fascinating.

All never to be solved.

Self-assured
smiling man,
Walking strong
through trouble
and woe.
Inner peace
calms the soul.

Mysterious human,

Keeping your knowledge locked inside.

Trapped into loneliness.

Straight thinking rigid man;

Direct to the point, any point—

No adjectives needed.

Small smile for the planet.

You have suffered the curse of mankind,

And still you keep spinning.

*What are you feeling?*
*Are your feelings written all over your face?*


Use the next few pages
just as you like.
Draw a face. Write a poem.
Or do both.

---◆---

## *Acknowledgments*

To Addie Bass whose stimulating four-line paintings inspired my work.

To the many people who encouraged me along the way.

To Dan Engelhardt who saw in the *FacePoems* a book or books which would bring joy to people.

To Richard Kelley who had the skills to take the *FacePoems* from the gallery wall and make them a book.

Lastly, and maybe firstly, the Buddha that fell off the wall in New Zealand.

# About the Artist

Fred Wallace lives in New Haven, Connecticut. He received a Ph.D. in political sociology from the University of Connecticut.

Never formally trained, he persisted in his writings, poetry, and artwork—developing a unique style focusing on the commonality of the human experience that soon gained widespread recognition and acclaim, winning *Best Poem* in a City of New Haven poetry contest.

His photo-montages have been exhibited in New Haven and Los Angeles. He has taught poetry at various Conferences in Connecticut and in New Zealand and published three volumes of poetry in the early 2000s. He is also the author of *A Well that Keeps Flowing*—exploring the theory and practice of self-help therapy—Co-Counseling (CCI).

He has finished and is looking to publish a book of historical fiction: *MAYDAY, 1971—A Generation's Last Battle Against the War in Vietnam*.

His life-long devotion to his creative mind and spirit has sustained and invigorated his life.

*Contact the Author at:*

earthfred@aol.com

www.ingramcontent.com/pod-product-compliance
Lightning Source LLC
Chambersburg PA
CBHW071935020426
42331CB00010B/2885